THE HISTORY OF MARINES AROUND THE WORLD

THE HISTORY OF MARINES AROUND THE WORLD

EDITED BY SHALINI SAXENA
SUPPLEMENTAL MATERIAL BY ADAM AUGUSTYN

Britannica
Educational Publishing

IN ASSOCIATION WITH

ROSEN
EDUCATIONAL SERVICES

Published in 2014 by Britannica Educational Publishing (a trademark of Encyclopædia Britannica, Inc.) in association with The Rosen Publishing Group, Inc.
29 East 21st Street, New York, NY 10010

Copyright © 2014 by Encyclopædia Britannica, Inc. Britannica, Encyclopædia Britannica, and the Thistle logo are registered trademarks of Encyclopædia Britannica, Inc. All rights reserved.

Rosen Publishing materials copyright © 2014 The Rosen Publishing Group, Inc. All rights reserved.

Distributed exclusively by Rosen Publishing.
To see additional Britannica Educational Publishing titles, go to rosenpublishing.com

First Edition

Britannica Educational Publishing
J.E. Luebering: Director, Core Reference Group
Anthony L. Green: Editor, Compton's by Britannica

Rosen Publishing
Hope Lourie Killcoyne: Executive Editor
Shalini Saxena: Editor
Nelson Sá: Art Director
Brian Garvey: Designer, Cover Design
Cindy Reiman: Photography Manager
Karen Huang: Photo Research
Introduction by Adam Augustyn

Cataloging-in-Publication Data

The history of marines around the world/editor, Shalini Saxena ; introduction and supplementary material by Adam Augustyn.
    pages cm.—(The world's armed forces)
Includes bibliographical references and index.
ISBN 978-1-62275-148-8 (library bound)
 1. Marines—History—Juvenile literature. 2. United States. Marine Corps—History—Juvenile literature.
I. Saxena, Shalini, 1982- editor. II. Augustyn, Adam, 1979- author of introduction.
VE15.H56 2014
359.9'609—dc23

2013036133

Manufactured in the United States of America

On the cover: (Top) American and South Korean marines participating in a joint landing operation in South Korea. *Chung Sung-Jun/Getty Images*. (Bottom left) Russian Marines standing at attention during an official ceremony. *Mahmud Turkia/AFP/Getty Images*. (Bottom right) A joint landing operation between American and South Korean marines in Pohang, South Korea. *Chung Sung-Jun/Getty Images*.

Cover and interior pages (camouflage pattern) © iStockphoto.com/EvgeniyDzhulay

CONTENTS

INTRODUCTION	8
CHAPTER 1: WHAT IS A MARINE CORPS?	13
Development	13
Galley Warfare	15
Command Structure	17
CHAPTER 2: EARLIEST MARINE CORPS	19
Byzantine Empire	19
Spain and Portugal	21
Royal Marines	23
The Royal Netherlands Corps Mariniers	26
Michiel Adriaanszoon de Ruyter	28
CHAPTER 3: MAJOR MILITARY ENGAGEMENTS THROUGH THE 19TH CENTURY	30
American Revolution	30
Great Siege of Gibraltar	31
Napoleonic Wars	34
Royal Marines Battalions	35
American Civil War	36
CHAPTER 4: MAJOR MILITARY ENGAGEMENTS FROM THE EARLY 20TH CENTURY THROUGH THE PRESENT	39
Banana Wars	39
World War I	41
Gallipoli Campaign	42
World War II	44
Korean War	47
Suez Crisis	48
Vietnam War	50
Falkland Islands War	52

Persian Gulf War   53
Afghanistan War   55
Iraq War   56

Chapter 5: Notable Marine Corps Around the World 58
China   58
France   60
The Netherlands   61
Russia   63
South Korea   65
United Kingdom   66
   Commando Training Centre Royal Marines   67

Chpater 6: The United States Marine Corps   70
Organization   70
   Recruit Training   72
   Women in the United States Marine Corps 75
   Semper Fidelis   77
Technology   78
   Vehicles   79
   Aircraft   81

Chapter 7: History of the United States Marine Corps 83
United States Marine Corps in the 19th Century   85
   Occupation of Haiti   87
United States Marine Corps in the Early 20th Century   88
   Battle of Belleau Wood   89
   Battle of Iwo Jima   91
United States Marine Corps from c. 1950 to c. 2000   93
   Lewis Puller   95
The United States Marine Corps in the Present   98

Conclusion   102
Glossary   103
For More Information   106
For Further Reading   110
Index   112

INTRODUCTION

The first organized military forces were, understandably, armies, as the earliest civilizations did not have the technology to fight on surfaces other than the land they occupied, making land-based warfare their only option. With the development of specialized warships, warfare moved to the seas with the advent of navies. The two forces met, in a way, with the establishment of marines, who first began service as naval infantries ready to attack the opposition—residing either on enemy ships or ashore—from sea vessels. The following pages will examine the development of marine corps around the world, their role in major military engagements, and the individuals who have helped make them into the extraordinary forces they are today.

The earliest marine corps were slight variations on naval battalions, with marines serving as infantry while in battle but as oarsmen or in other roles on a ship's crew while at sea. Modern marine corps came into being in the 17th century and rose to prominence during the major global conflicts of the 20th century, when amphibious warfare became

The U.S. Marine Corps War Memorial in Arlington, Va., at night. The memorial, designed after a famous photograph, depicts members of the United States Marines and Navy raising an American flag on the island of Iwo Jima after their success in this notable battle of World War II. Samuel Antonio/Flickr Vision/Getty Images

INTRODUCTION

central to many military campaigns and a strong corps was a fundamental component of a victorious military. (In fact, the most notorious war in the history of western civilization, World War II, is believed by many military historians to have been decided in no small part by Germany's inadequate amphibious capability.)

So what is amphibious warfare? Broadly defined, it consists of military operations

characterized by attacks launched from the sea by naval and landing forces against hostile shores. The main form is the amphibious assault, which may be conducted for any of several purposes: to serve as a prelude to further combat operations ashore; to seize a site required as an advanced naval or air base; or to deny the use of the site or area to the enemy. Landing of expeditionary forces on a shore or at a port already secured by friendly forces is not usually included in the concept.

Although ostensibly tied to their respective navies, marines across the globe today usually operate relatively independently as military forces in their own right. In fact, despite the name, marines are in many ways removed from an explicit connection to the sea. While landing operations are still inextricable features of corps, marines also regularly go to battle in the air and in landlocked battlegrounds. Where once ships were the defining marine corps transport, modern technology has made it possible to send marines into battle in—among other vehicles—amphibious landing crafts, tanks, helicopters, and jets, and has even led to occasionally removing the soldier entirely from confrontation, as in the case of unmanned drone aircraft.

INTRODUCTION

In recent years, the structure and demographics of marine corps around the world have changed drastically compared to the historic makeup of corps. The most noticeable change is, perhaps, the addition of women over the past century to what was an exclusively male enterprise since the earliest corps of the Byzantine Empire. Women primarily served clerical or other noncombat duties, but by the early 21st century they were playing full roles in all aspects of many marine corps throughout the world. Similarly, homosexual individuals were allowed to serve in dozens of marine corps worldwide by the mid-2010s, and the number of corps that allow openly homosexual soldiers to serve will surely grow in the approaching years.

No matter the advance in troop makeup, technological innovation, or other fundamental changes to marine corps in the future, one constant promises to be that their soldiers will be used in every way possible and will continue to prove themselves among the most versatile and tenacious of any fighting force on Earth.

WHAT IS A MARINE CORPS?

CHAPTER 1

Soldiers of the fleet is probably the best term to describe marines. They are troops recruited, trained, and organized for land, sea, and air service in operations related to naval campaigns. The word "marine" is derived from the Latin word *mare*, meaning "sea." The most significant exploits by such troops were probably during World War II, when fighting men of the United States Marine Corps were landed on island beaches throughout the Pacific theater of war. Their mission was to take control of island after island from occupying Japanese forces. They were normally the initial assault troops who established beachheads and engaged in some of the bloodiest combat of the war.

DEVELOPMENT

The use at sea of troops essentially trained for land warfare was a natural outgrowth of the way sea battles were fought for many centuries.

THE HISTORY OF MARINES AROUND THE WORLD

United States Marines trudging through mud on Bougainville Island before facing Japanese forces during World War II. Marines were instrumental in such campaigns in the Pacific throughout the war. Hulton Archive/Getty Images

During the long age of galley warfare, the ships sought direct confrontations. They used two basic tactics—ramming and boarding. If an enemy ship was not sunk by ramming, it was usually boarded by soldiers who had been specially trained to fight sea battles.

It was not until the 17th century, however, that there was any attempt to raise forces of men who were distinctly marines and not ordinary infantrymen. During the 1660s the

GALLEY WARFARE

Galley warfare is sea warfare fought between forces equipped with specialized oar-driven warships, particularly in the Mediterranean Sea, where it originated in antiquity and continued into the age of gunpowder.

Galley warfare in the Classical Mediterranean was based on the ram-equipped trireme, which reached its highest level of development in ancient Greece from the 5th to the 1st century BCE. Although boarding was also practiced, the main tactic was ramming. Ram-equipped triremes were extraordinarily nimble, and fleets of these vessels employed a variety of formations from which they could maneuver to ram and disable other ships. During the Hellenistic period, very large galleys were used mainly—though not exclusively—as platforms for missile weapons and boarding. Once Rome had achieved control of the Mediterranean, galleys

An ancient Greek trireme, a galley with three banks of oars, used during the age of galley warfare. Hulton Archive/Getty Images

GALLEY WARFARE (CONTINUED)

became fewer and smaller. During the Dark Ages the ram was abandoned, and boarding to capture became the dominant tactic.

In the second golden age of Mediterranean galley warfare, from about 1200 to the mid-1600s, the galleys were rowed by oarsmen on a single level on the upper deck, rather than in multiple tiers with some of the oarsmen below decks as was common in antiquity. Cannon-armed galleys dominated war at sea in the Mediterranean until the early 1600s, occasionally venturing into the English Channel, and they were used in the Red Sea, Persian Gulf, and Caribbean and Indian waters. In the 1540s war galleys were introduced into the Baltic Sea, where they were used into the 18th century.

Dutch and English both organized the first modern corps of marines. It was at this time that the word "marine" first came into use to describe these soldiers.

As firepower gained ascendancy, the occurrence of actual infantry-type combat on ships became far less frequent. Today it has virtually disappeared. Marines are now mainly land and air fighters, though they are attached to navies and need the support of ships for coastal assaults and supplies.

Command Structure

Although marine forces are still under the authority of navy departments, their grades and ranks are more similar to those of an army. The ranks listed here are those of the United States Marine Corps. As with the other military branches, members of the Marine Corps are divided into enlisted men and commissioned officers. Among the enlisted men there are several ranks of noncommissioned officers. A recruit enters the marines as a private, equal to a seaman recruit. The first level of advancement is private first class, on a level with seaman apprentice. Above this rank is lance corporal, the equivalent of private first class in the Army. Then, in order, come corporal, sergeant, staff sergeant, gunnery sergeant, first sergeant or master sergeant, and sergeant major or master gunnery sergeant.

The commissioned officers range from warrant officer up to four-star general. As in the other service branches, the warrant officer is a rank reached by noncommissioned officers after special training. It is, for most of those who hold it, a permanent rank throughout a military career. Those who possess it

THE HISTORY OF MARINES AROUND THE WORLD

A recruiter of the United States Marines speaking to students about service in the Corps. Recruiters provide information to individuals who wish to know more about joining the Marines. Mary Knox Merrill/Christian Science Monitor/Getty Images

are well-trained specialists such as helicopter pilots, and their pay scale rises in accordance with length of service. Within the rank there are five grades, depending on length of service.

The ranks of the other commissioned officers are comparable to the Army: second lieutenant, first lieutenant, captain, major, lieutenant colonel, colonel, brigadier general, major general, lieutenant general, and general. There is no five-star rank for generals in the Marine Corps as there is in the Army and Air Force.

EARLIEST MARINE CORPS

CHAPTER 2

The use of marines goes far back in history. The 5th-century-BCE Greek historians Herodotus and Thucydides referred to *epibatai*, or heavy-armed sea soldiers in the Greek fleets, while Polybius, in the 3rd–2nd century BCE, described *milites classiarii* ("soldiers of the fleet"), a category of Roman soldier organized and specially armed for duty aboard warships. During the Middle Ages, ordinary soldiers in Europe were frequently embarked aboard ship to provide a fighting backbone, but not until the naval wars of the 17th century was the distinct and organized role of marines almost simultaneously rediscovered by the British and Dutch, who raised the first two modern corps of marines—the Royal Marines (1664) and the Koninklijke Nederlandse Corps Mariniers (1665), respectively.

BYZANTINE EMPIRE

The marines of the Byzantine Empire served onboard the numerous warships of the

THE HISTORY OF MARINES AROUND THE WORLD

A statue of Thucydides, an ancient Greek historian who wrote about armed soldiers in the Greek sea fleets, some of the first known marines.
ppl/Shutterstock.com

empire's powerful fleet, where they served as infantry on landing parties and during ship-to-ship combat. At sea during galley warfare, Byzantine ships would either ram an enemy vessel or, in later years, pull up towards a ship and establish contact via a specialized beakhead attached to the bow, and marines would cross over and invade the enemy ship. Later marines would launch missiles towards the enemy in an effort to weaken and demoralize them before boarding their ships. The most effective missile in the marines' arsenal was "Greek fire," a flammable substance invented in the 7th century CE that set fire to enemy ships and was a particularly important factor in terrifying and repelling the Muslim fleet in sieges of Constantinople from the early 8th century on.

Spain and Portugal

The history of the Spanish marines is inextricably linked with one of the most famed military forces of all time: the Spanish Armada. Charles V, the king of Spain, created the Infanteria de Marina (Spanish Marine Infantry) in 1537 to serve as the manpower for the country's massive fleet of warships.

At over 475 years old, the Infanteria is the oldest continuously functioning amphibious force in the world.

The early Infanteria made its most famous historical contribution during the Armada's attempted invasion of England in 1588. The Spanish king at the time, Philip II, wanted to restore Roman Catholicism in England and exact a measure of revenge on the English pirates who had been attacking Spanish trade ships. Philip sent 130 ships and nearly 30,000 troops across the English Channel. The intimidating sea force was met by long-range attacks from English naval forces and after a series of engagements that took place over several weeks, the English forces were able to defeat the famed Armada, which returned to Spain with only 60 ships. The English victory was integral to cementing Protestantism as the religion of that country, as the repelling of the Catholic Armada was seen by many English as a manifestation of (the Protestant) God's will.

Spain's Iberian neighbor Portugal also created a nascent marine corps in the 16th century. Portuguese soldiers of the fleet (Infantes de Marinha) began overseeing the transport of goods on ships bound for India in 1585. The official founding of the Portuguese Marine Corps (Corpo de Fuzileiros) dates to 1621, when the Marines came into existence as the Terço (specialized infantry) of the Portuguese Navy. While not as storied as the Spanish Marines, the Corpo de Fuzileiros served in important maritime battles during its first centuries of existence, particularly in Brazil, Portugal's most important overseas colony.

Royal Marines

Great Britain's Royal Marines were founded on Oct. 26, 1664, as a regiment of 1,200 "land soldiers prepared for sea service." The word "royal" was not actually used to designate the force until 1802 during the Napoleonic wars. From 1664 until 1775 the various marine regiments underwent several reorganizations and disbandments, and their control alternated between the Admiralty and the Army. The most distinguished episode of this period was the capture and control of Gibraltar on the southern tip of Spain in 1704–05.

In 1755 the Corps of Marines was reorganized into 50 companies and grouped into three divisions—all under Admiralty control. The divisions were based at Chatham,

Rendering of the British Siege of Gibraltar in 1704. Rischgitz/Hulton Archive/Getty Images

Portsmouth, and Plymouth. This organization endured until 1947 with some modifications. In 1805 a fourth division was added, based at Woolwich, and an artillery company was added to each division. The Woolwich division was disbanded in 1869. In 1855 the Corps was divided into infantry and artillery companies, each with its own designation. This separation ended in 1923, and the Corps was reconstituted as the Royal Marines.

Royal Marines dressed as 17th-century marines during St. George's Day celebrations in 1929, six years after the Corps was united. Planet News Archive/SSPL/Getty Images

The Royal Marines served with distinction in the Seven Years' War (1756–63), the American Revolution, the Napoleonic wars, and the Crimean War. In World War I they appeared in nearly every area of combat on land and sea. There were 6,000 marines present at Jutland, the largest sea battle of the war. They also took part in some of the hardest fighting in France during four years of stalemated trench warfare. During World

War II the marines attained a top strength of 78,000. They were in service around the world from Europe to the Far East. They took part in the losing defense of Singapore against the Japanese, an episode in which very few survived. One commando unit was sent to Korea in 1950 and served with the United States First Marine Division. Six years later marines took part in the assault on the Suez Canal during a conflict with Egypt.

The Royal Netherlands Corps Mariniers

The Koninklijke Nederlandse Corps Mariniers (Royal Netherlands Marine Corps) was founded by Admiral Michiel Adriaanszoon de Ruyter and Johan de Witt, the councillor pensionary (political leader) of Holland, in 1665 during the Second Anglo-Dutch War (1665–67). The establishment of the Corps Mariniers during a war with England was not coincidental—the two countries had the greatest navies in the world in the 17th century and the Corps helped extend their rivalry for maritime domination into the 18th century.

The Corps' first major battle— the Raid on the Medway—took place, naturally, during the Second Anglo-Dutch War. That battle saw the Dutch Navy begin to boldly sail up England's River Medway towards a shipyard based in Chatham on June 10, 1667. Within a week the Navy—with vital support from troops of the newly formed Corps—had destroyed 13 English ships, which proved to be the decisive moment in the war, as England sued for peace soon thereafter.

The two counties again went to war five years later. A key battle of the Third Anglo-Dutch War was the Battle of Solebay ("Solebay" is shorthand for Southwold Bay) on May 28, 1672. In it, the Dutch Marines again attacked England but this time the target was Southwold, where much of the combined Anglo-French fleet was on shore leave. The allied countries managed to repel the surprise attack, but not before the Dutch forces destroyed two ships and caused 2,000 casualties in the course of a day. The fighting ended with both sides claiming victory, but the Dutch attack caused enough damage that England and France were forced to abandon a plan to

THE HISTORY OF MARINES AROUND THE WORLD

MICHIEL ADRIAANSZOON DE RUYTER

A statue of Michiel Adriaanszoon de Ruyter in the Netherlands. Wil Tilroe-Otte/Shutterstock.com

Michiel Adriaanszoon de Ruyter (1607–76) was one of the Netherlands' greatest admirals. His brilliant naval victories in the Second and Third Anglo-Dutch wars enabled the United Provinces to maintain a balance of power with England.

Employed at sea at the age of nine, De Ruyter by 1635 had become a merchant captain. After serving as rear admiral of a Dutch fleet assisting Portugal against Spain in 1641, he returned to the merchant service for the next 10 years, fighting against the Barbary pirates off the north African coast. With the outbreak of the First Anglo-Dutch War (1652–54), he accepted a naval command, serving with distinction under Maarten Tromp and attaining the rank of vice admiral in 1653 after his victory off Texel.

In 1659 De Ruyter supported Denmark against Sweden in the Baltic in the First Northern War (1655–60). He fought against the English (1664–65) off the Guinea Coast of Africa, helping to restore the Dutch West India Company's commercial dominance in the area, but he was unsuccessful in subsequent campaigns against the English in the West Indies.

Returning to the United Provinces in 1665, De Ruyter was named lieutenant admiral of Holland and worked closely with Johan De Witt to strengthen the Dutch navy and create the Corps Mariniers. In the Second Anglo-Dutch War (1665–67), his greatest victories were in the Four Days' Battle (June 1666) and in the raid on the Medway (June 1667), in which much of the English fleet was destroyed; the latter victory accelerated the Anglo-Dutch peace negotiations that had begun at Breda in April 1667.

De Ruyter's performance in the Third Anglo-Dutch War (1672–74) has been considered his greatest achievement: his victories over larger Anglo-French forces off Solebay (1672) and Ostend and Kijkduin (1673) prevented an invasion of the Dutch Republic from the sea. In 1675–76 he fought against the French in the Mediterranean and was mortally wounded off Sicily.

blockade Dutch trade routes. As the power of the Dutch navy faded during the 18th century owing to losses in wars and decreased Dutch commercial influence, the Corps' prestige also faded.

CHAPTER 3

MAJOR MILITARY ENGAGEMENTS THROUGH THE 19TH CENTURY

While the concept of a "marine" was still relatively new in the 18th and 19th centuries, those forces made significant impacts on global warfare throughout those eras. England's Royal Marines were the dominant marine force almost since the day the branch was founded, but by the turn of the 20th century their American counterparts began their ascent to the top of the worldwide marine hierarchy.

AMERICAN REVOLUTION

Marine involvement in the American Revolution (1775–83) consisted of both the overseas deployment of the Royal Marines and, more significantly, the creation of the United States Marine Corps. The American Corps was formed in direct reaction to the presence of the British Marines. The earliest American Marines to take part in the war effort were actually affiliated with their respective states until the creation of the Corps in November 1775.

The duties of members of the Continental Marine Corps during the Revolution consisted primarily of service on ships of the United States Navy. Marines most commonly engaged British troops by being stationed in the tops of masts and shooting at the enemy (many of the Marines were excellent shots). Although their roles as sharpshooters in naval engagements had obvious import, American Marines were rarely at the forefront of important Revolution battles; instead, they often participated in landing parties, were stationed in forts, guarded prisoners, and served in expeditionary forces. Conversely, the Royal Marines were integral to the British victory in the Battle of Bunker Hill (June 17, 1775), where a Marine Force under Major John Pitcairn took part in the successful capture of the hill despite the deaths of 29 Marines and injuries to 87 more.

Great Siege of Gibraltar

On June 24, 1779, the largest action (in terms of numbers) of the American Revolution began, but it took place over

George Augustus Elliott, a British military officer during the Great Siege of Gibraltar and a governor of Gibraltar, with the keys of Gibraltar. Universal Images Group/Getty Images

3,000 miles east of the United States. Sensing an opportunity to take advantage of Britain's increased North American military presence, Spain and France laid siege to the British territory of Gibraltar, which is located on a narrow peninsula of Spain's southern Mediterranean coast and which England had possessed since 1704. Gibraltar had been besieged numerous times in its history, no matter which country claimed the territory. In addition to the strategic importance of Gibraltar as access to the Mediterranean Sea, Britain viewed it as an important symbol of its naval strength, and the attempted siege was met with fierce resistance.

The Great Siege began with a combined Franco-Spanish naval blockade of the seas surrounding Gibraltar alongside a military build-up on the thin strip of land connecting Gibraltar to mainland Spain. This attempt to starve the garrison of 5,382 British troops was joined by attacks from land and sea. The British soldiers—primarily consisting of Royal Marines—endured an outbreak of scurvy in addition to the onslaught. The garrison was relieved by British ships that broke through the blockade in 1780 and 1781 to provide much-needed supplies and reinforcements. Britain ultimately staved off the assault after three years and seven months, making it the longest siege endured in the history of the British Armed Forces.

THE HISTORY OF MARINES AROUND THE WORLD

NAPOLEONIC WARS

The Napoleonic wars (1803–15) were a series of wars between France (under the leadership of Napoleon Bonaparte) and a shifting alliance of other European powers. The most prominent marine units to take part in the wars were from what was then the dominant marine force in the world, Britain's Royal Marines. Within three years of war again being declared between the two longstanding enemies in 1803, the

A ship-of-the-line of the Royal Navy during the Napoleonic wars. Royal Marines served alongside members of the Royal Navy throughout the conflict. Rischgitz/Hulton Archive/Getty Images

Royal Marines almost tripled its fighting force to over 31,000 men. The Royal Marines took part in every major sea conflict during the Napoleonic wars—often serving interchangeably with troops of the British Navy—including the Battle of Trafalgar (October 21, 1805), which established British Naval (and therefore Marine) superiority for more than 100 years.

ROYAL MARINES BATTALIONS

During the Napoleonic wars, the Royal Marines formed three battalions to be deployed overseas. The 1st Battalion was formed in 1810 to fight in Lisbon and, later, in North America during the War of 1812. The 2nd Battalion was created in 1812 and served primarily in northern Spain before also moving to North America. In 1814 the Marines created the 3rd Battalion, which fought in the Netherlands and North America. While in North America, each of the three battalions consisted of six infantry companies and one artillery company and the battalions fought in every theatre of the War of 1812 except for the Northwest. Unlike previous Royal Marine battalions, which were temporary and formed impromptu from standing Marine units, these were noteworthy for being the first semi-permanent battalions in Royal Marine history.

American Civil War

While the American Civil War (1861–65) is most often associated with brutal land engagements fought by the respective combatant's armies and bloody battlefields, marines from both the Union and Confederate sides played a role (if relatively minor) in the warfare. The most significant marine contribution to the Civil War actually took place before the war broke out when, on Oct. 18, 1859, a group of 86 United States Marines attacked the abolitionist John Brown and his supporters at Harpers Ferry, Va., where Brown's group had captured a federal armory in an effort to establish a stronghold for freed slaves. The Marines' attack—which resulted in the deaths of seventeen men and the capture of Brown and his remaining six followers, who were all later executed—and the resulting fallout greatly increased the tensions between slaveholding and non-slaveholding states, accelerating the path to civil war.

When the war broke out, the United States Marine Corps was greatly weakened by the defections of enlisted men and officers who joined the Confederate cause. Attempts

MAJOR MILITARY ENGAGEMENTS THROUGH THE 19TH CENTURY

In 1859 John Brown's raid on the Harpers Ferry arsenal was blocked by Marines who surrounded the raiders in an engine house and forced their surrender. Interim Archives/Archive Photos/Getty Images

to build up the Corps were limited by the prioritization of increasing the number of Army soldiers, and Union Marines primarily served as ship guards during the war. However, Union Marines did participate in the Navy's unsuccessful landing operation at Fort Fisher (Jan. 13–14, 1865) and earned honors for their service on gun crews aboard ships. A Confederate Marine Corps was created on March 16, 1861, and—like its Union counterpart—its members served mostly on the ships of the Confederate Navy.

MAJOR MILITARY ENGAGEMENTS FROM THE EARLY 20TH CENTURY THROUGH THE PRESENT

By becoming, along with the Soviet Union, one of the two global superpowers during the 20th century, the United States increased its military presence throughout the world during that century, with the Marine Corps playing a prominent role. While the Soviet military did not emphasize the role of marines in its institutional structure, the United States certainly did, and the American naval infantry became one of the most respected (and feared) fighting forces on the globe.

Banana Wars

The so-called Banana Wars were not actually proper wars. Instead, the term is used to refer to a number of military actions the United States instigated in various Central American and Caribbean countries from

1898 to 1934. The actions were almost always carried out by the United States Marine Corps, often to protect American corporate interests in fruit companies from the leftist governments of those countries that were seeking to increase national control of the industries, giving rise to the name Banana Wars. The Marines' activities in the Banana Wars went a long way in establishing the lasting reputation of the Corps as a top-flight counterinsurgency force that can operate in relative secrecy.

The first Banana War came with the beginning of the Spanish-American War when the U.S. invaded Spain-controlled Cuba, but it was primarily a naval operation. The Marine Corps' involvement in the Banana Wars began with an invasion of Panama in 1903, and the Corps subsequently sent troops to, among other countries, Nicaragua, Haiti, and Honduras in the following decades. In fact, the Marines had so much experience fighting in the region that, in 1935, the Corps published the book *Small Wars Operations* (now called the *Small Wars Manual*), which details the new fighting techniques—such as anti-guerilla actions and small-scale sea-based international intervention—that the Marines developed during the Banana Wars.

World War I

Marines from both the Allies and Central Powers played relatively minor, but integral, roles in the war efforts of their countries during World War I (1914–18). Early in the war, Britain's Royal Marines took part in the defense of Antwerp, Belgium, (where they were met by the German Marines equivalent, the Seebataillon) and the Gallipoli Campaign.

The Royal Marines took part in a raid on the German-occupied Belgian port of Zeebrugge on the night of April 22–23, 1918. Zeebrugge was integral to the German war effort, as the port was the site of a U-boat base and was a threat to Allied shipping lines due to its proximity to the English Channel. The raid began with heavy artillery fire from British battleships offshore in an attempt to create a smokescreen for a landing party of some 200 Royal Marines. The party drew German fire, which allowed the Royal Navy to sink three ships to blockade the port. Despite the much heavier casualty count on the British side, the Allies declared the raid a success for the major disruption it created for the German sea force.

GALLIPOLI CAMPAIGN

The Gallipoli Campaign (also known as the Dardanelles Campaign) was one of the key battles in World War I. Turkey's strategically important Dardanelles channel (the 38-mile [61-km] long strait where the Aegean Sea meets the Sea of Marmara that stands in the way of southern access to Istanbul) had long been considered one of the most impenetrable seaways in the world. British authorities had pondered invading the Dardanelles earlier in the 20th century and were met with resistance from the military, but when war broke out between the Allies and Turkey, the mission—while still dangerous—was

Allied troops on the Gallipoli Peninsula during the Gallipoli Campaign of World War I. Hulton Archive/Getty Images

reclassified as both possible and integral to the Allied war effort.

On April 25, 1915, British, Australian, and New Zealander Marines landed on the Gallipoli Peninsula on the north side of the Dardanelles. (A French contingent landed on the southern side of the strait but was quickly withdrawn.) The Allies made minor progress but were mostly kept pinned to the beaches by Turkish troops and experienced heavy casualties over many months. The disastrous Gallipoli Campaign became a hot-button political issue in Britain as it led to the resignation of then-Lord of the Admiralty Winston Churchill and was a major contributor to the supersession of Prime Minister H.H. Asquith's Liberal administration before the last of the Allied troops were withdrawn in January 1916. Among the many military lessons learned from the campaign were that future Marine invasions must act with as much secrecy and speed as possible (Turkish troops were well-aware of the pending invasion and had plenty of time to amass a defensive force) and use transport ships that are combat-ready.

The United States Marine Corps was heavily involved in the Battle of Blanc Mont Ridge, which took place from Oct. 3–27, 1918. Two Marine infantry brigades worked in concert with the French Fourth Army to converge on the German defenses. After weeks of fighting, the Allies managed to reach their goal, which resulted in the

German Army being forced completely out of France's Champagne region, which they had controlled for four years.

World War II

World War II was something of a coming-out party for marine corps throughout the world. Since Marines are a relatively new fighting force compared to Navies and Armies, they were not large parts of a country's military actions until improved technology, increased manpower, and strategic opportunity all came together in the Second World War.

With fronts in the water-surrounded European peninsula and in the Pacific Ocean, there were plenty of battle locales that called for naval infantrymen. Nearly every major power involved in the war utilized marines, who fought in such signature battles as the attack on Pearl Harbor, the Battles of Guadalcanal and Iwo Jima, and the Normandy Invasion. On the Axis side, Germany infantry members of the Kriegsmarine (German Navy) fought in numerous battles, but their actions were primarily tied with those of the Navy so their status as a distinct marine branch is questionable. Russian and French

An amphibious tractor transporting marines across a beach during World War II. Such amphibious vehicles were an important part of marine engagements throughout the war. Dmitri Kessel/Time & Life Pictures/ Getty Images

Marines saw limited action in World War II, so the marine contribution to the Allied cause was primarily made by Britain's Royal Marines and, most famously, the United States Marine Corps.

The Royal Marines took part in many of Britain's naval operations, but also participated in amphibious raiding parties and piloted aircrafts. But what they are best known for are their many daring amphibious landings, particularly the Allied invasions of Sicily and Normandy. The Normandy Invasion (also known as D-Day) was launched on June 6, 1944, and was the first strike in the liberation of France and eventual defeat of Germany. At Normandy, some 17,000 Royal Marines were a part of the forces that landed on the beaches during the invasion, which was by far the largest Royal Marine effort of the war.

The United States Marine Corps had its most famous battle in the Pacific Theatre during World War II. Marines were part of the defensive force that vainly tried to fight off the Japanese raid on Pearl Harbor that brought the United States into the war. Additionally two Marine divisions took part in the last major land battle of the war, the Battle of Okinawa. One of the Corps' most acclaimed actions during the years in between was the Battle of Guadalcanal, wherein 6,000 Marines spearheaded the assault on the Japanese-held island of Guadalcanal in the South Pacific. After six months of bitter fighting in the island's jungles, the U.S. forces prevailed in what became—along with the naval victory at the Battle of Midway—the turning point in the Pacific War.

Korean War

In the wake of World War II, the United States Marine Corps was greatly reduced in size, but it was built up again when the United States entered the Korean War (1950–53). The Marine Corps was a key component to the U.S. military effort to support South Korea (at the behest of the United Nations [UN]) against the Soviet Union- and China-backed North. Nearly 250,000 Marines served in Korea, many of whom were front-line troops along the 38th parallel (the boundary between the two Korean nations), where the conflict stagnated into a war of attrition over time.

One of the most significant actions of the war was the daring surprise landing at Inch'ŏn on the west coast of the Korean peninsula near Seoul. On Sept. 15, 1950, the 1st Marine Division, along with the United States Army's 7th Infantry Division and South Korean troops, landed amidst the worst tidal conditions the Marines had ever faced and pinched off an attempted North Korean invasion from the rear and re-captured Seoul within two weeks. The most storied Marine maneuver of the war was the battle of the Chosin Reservoir, where in November and December of 1950 the 1st Marine Division turned back on a massive attack of Chinese forces and fought their way down a narrow vulnerable road through several mountain passes and a bridged chasm until they reached transport ships waiting at the coast. While the Korean War ended with no clear "winner," it was nevertheless noteworthy in Marine Corps history for the Corps' first use of helicopters and jets in combat.

Suez Crisis

The Suez Crisis was precipitated by Egyptian president Gamal Abdel Nasser when he suddenly nationalized the Suez Canal on July 26, 1956. The canal had been owned by British and French interests since it was built. After diplomatic attempts to solve the crisis failed, France and Britain allied with Israel—who was long opposed to the Nasser regime—and Israeli forces launched an attack on Egypt on Oct. 29, 1956. The Israeli offensive gave the French and British governments the cover they needed to demand an end to hostilities and enter the fray under the auspices of a UN-ordered cease fire, but with the secret goal of regaining control of the canal and possibly ousting Nasser.

On November 5, a joint Anglo-French Marine landing force came ashore at Egypt's Port Said. They were supplemented by Royal Marine commandos who made history's first helicopter-borne assault landing. However, the presumed superiority of the Anglo-French forces was undermined by fierce resistance from the Egyptian military, and little progress was made before political and economic pressures forced the European nations to acquiesce to U.S.-sponsored UN resolutions and withdraw from Egypt. This ultimately led to the loss of most of the two countries' influence in the Middle East.

Vietnam War

The Vietnam War (1954–75) was fought between the two sides of the formerly united country, which split apart into the communist-controlled North Vietnam and the democratic South Vietnam following the end of French colonial rule in 1954. The United States aided and fought alongside the South while the Soviet Union and China supplied the North with weapons, supplies, and advisers. The United States Marine Corps entered the war with the rest of the American fighting forces in 1965, initially sending just two battalions to Vietnam.

As the war progressed, many more Marines joined the fight and troops from the Corps took part in many of the war's most notable battles, such as Da Nang and Khe Sanh. The Marines largest battle in Vietnam took place at Hue during the Tet Offensive (the surprise North Vietnamese offensive that took place during the cease-fire for the national Tet holiday). Over the course of a 25-day battle that destroyed much of the city, the South Vietnamese Army and U.S. forces including three Marine Corps battalions (who incurred 1,200 casualties total) defeated 10,000

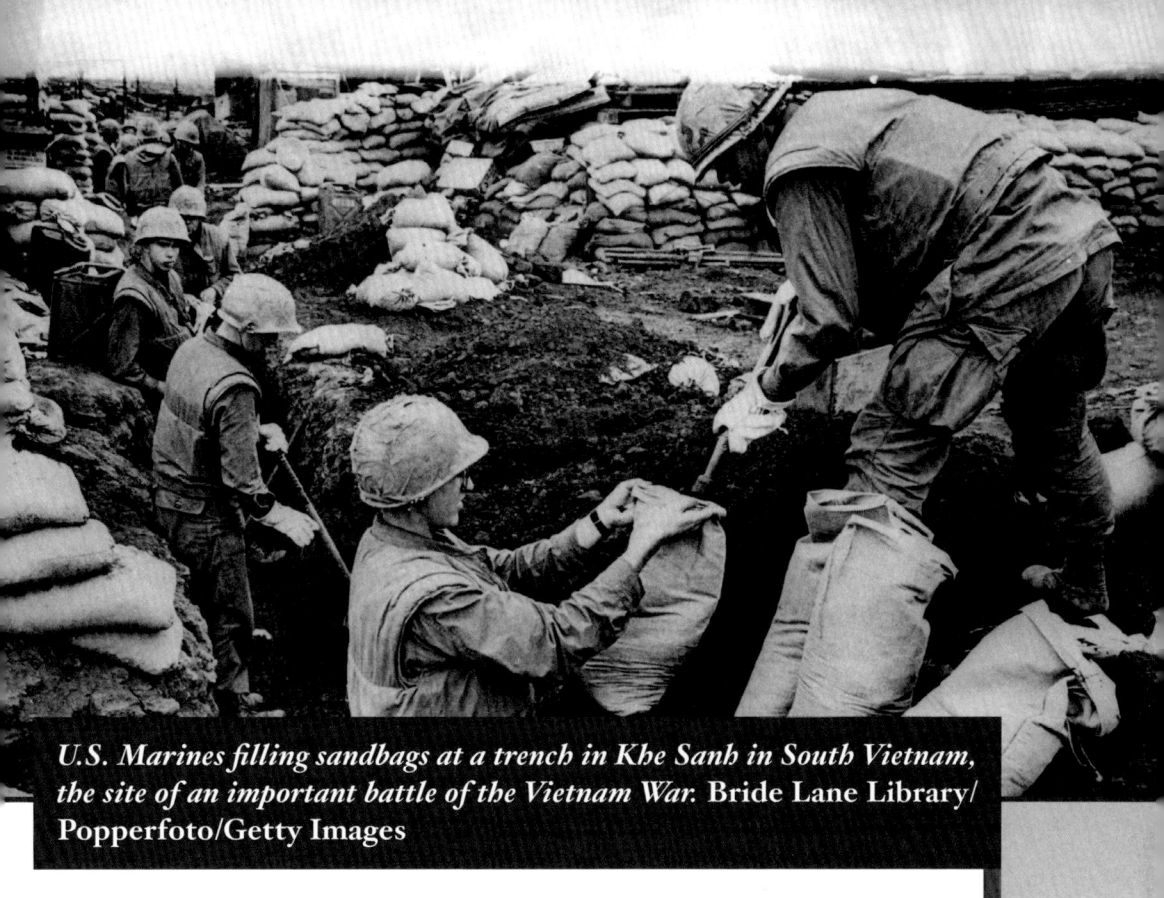

U.S. Marines filling sandbags at a trench in Khe Sanh in South Vietnam, the site of an important battle of the Vietnam War. Bride Lane Library/Popperfoto/Getty Images

North Vietnamese troops for one of the few clear South Vietnam/U.S. victories of the protracted and chaotic war.

In addition to service along the front lines, one of the most important roles for Marines was service as a "Recon" Marine, which involved troops being dropped off via helicopter in remote areas of the Vietnamese jungle, where they fought off hidden enemies and gathered intelligence integral to the American war effort.

Falkland Islands War

The Falkland Islands War was a brief undeclared war fought between Argentina and Great Britain from April 2 to June 14, 1982, over control of the Falkland Islands and associated island dependencies off the coast of Argentina. The war began when the Argentine military invaded the islands (which had been under British control since 1833) and overran a small garrison of British troops. The British military sent a naval task force built around two aircraft carriers to re-take the islands, and after two months of pitched battles they managed to do so.

One of the most impressive feats in the history of the Royal Marines took place during the war, although it was only made public in 2009. Soon after the war began, an Argentine invasion force of hundreds of soldiers attempted to take South Georgia, an island approximately 960 miles (1,500 km) east of the Falklands. They were met by a defensive force of just 22 Royal Marines, who, using only small arms, managed to cripple an Argentine warship off of the coast and repel the invasion with enough tenacity that the Argentine military leaders were forced to agree to safe transport home for the British soldiers before the island was ultimately surrendered to the overwhelming Argentine force.

Persian Gulf War

The Persian Gulf War (1990–91) saw the United States Marine Corps' first large-scale action in a generation. After Iraq invaded its small, oil-rich neighbor Kuwait on August 2, 1990, the United Nations put together a coalition of 700,000 troops (540,000 from the United States) for a planned attack to force Iraq out. The attack, code-named "Operation Desert Storm" began on Jan. 17, 1991, with Marine and Navy aviators joining a bombing campaign that has been called the "most powerful and successful air assault in the history of modern warfare." The signature Marine Corps action of the war was the Liberation of Kuwait, which was launched on Feb. 24, 1991. The 1st and 2nd Marine Divisions (each with over 18,000 troops) led the ground attack into Kuwait through sand berms, two minefields, miles of barbed

A U.S. Marine holding position outside of the U.S. Embassy in Kuwait City during the Persian Gulf War, while a Marine helicopter flies overhead. Bob Pearson/AFP/Getty Images

wire, and sporadic Iraqi artillery assaults to retake Kuwait City in just three days.

The Royal Marines also played key roles in the Gulf War, participating in a number of combat and humanitarian missions in Iraq and the surrounding areas.

AFGHANISTAN WAR

The Afghanistan War (2001–), one of the longest conflicts in American history, was initiated by the September 11 terrorist attacks and the U.S. government's subsequent desire to topple the Taliban, the ultraconservative political and religious faction that ruled Afghanistan and provided sanctuary for al-Qaeda, perpetrators of the attacks. United States Marine Corps units were the first conventional fighting forces to enter Afghanistan in November 2001. The following month, Marine soldiers captured the strategically important Kandahār International Airport, which was then turned into a base for coalition forces. After the ouster of the Taliban government two months after the invasion began, Marines stayed on to fight off the remnants of the Taliban fighters and to train Afghani troops.

U.S. Marines patrolling a remote part of the Helmand Province of Afghanistan. Scott Olson/Getty Images

Iraq War

The United States Marine Corps returned to Iraq 12 years after the end of the Persian Gulf War. In the Iraq War (2003–11), Marines from the U.S. and Britain were tasked with contributing to the overthrow of the government of President Ṣaddām Ḥussein. The soldiers of the American 1st Marine Expeditionary Force were among the first to invade Iraq in March 2003. Members of the Marine Corps also fought in the Battle of Fallujah in November and December 2004, wherein Regimental Combat Team 1 and Regimental Combat Team 7 of the Corps fought in what was arguably the fiercest combat the Corps had seen since the Vietnam War. The coalition forces emerged victorious in that battle, but endured over 650 casualties in so doing.

During the early stages of the war, the 2,000 troops of the Royal Marines' 3rd Commando Brigade joined their American counterparts in participating in assault landings as well as the intense urban warfare that secured the cities of Umm Qaṣr, Basra, and others.

CHAPTER 5

NOTABLE MARINE CORPS AROUND THE WORLD

The modern United States Marine Corps is one of the largest marine forces in the world and has notably served in a number of conflicts around the world. But many other countries also maintain maritime combat troops. While the command structures, duties, and culture of these corps may vary widely, they are nevertheless united by the simple fact of being marines.

China

While home to one of the world's oldest civilizations, China has only recently created a standalone unit of marines. With the communist revolution came the creation of the People's Liberation Army (PLA), who, in turn, formed China's first modern naval infantry in April 1953: the People's Liberation Army Navy Marine Corps. The Corps was formed to conduct amphibious operations against

NOTABLE MARINE CORPS AROUND THE WORLD

The People's Liberation Army Navy Marine Corps marching in a parade through Tiananmen Square in Beijing, China. ChinaFotoPress/Getty Images

islands held by the Chinese Nationalist Party, but with the dissolution of this goal the Corps was disbanded in October 1957. An infantry force composed solely of Navy personnel continued to serve as China's de facto Marines until the PLA revived the Corps in 1980. As currently construed, the PLA Navy Marine Corps contains about 12,000 troops in two brigades that are part of the Navy's South Sea Fleet.

The island of Taiwan (home of the Nationalist Chinese government that fled the mainland after China's turn to communism) operates a separate marine corps, the Republic of China Marine Corps, which primarily serves to defend Taiwan and its territories from incursions by the PLA.

France

Despite being the home of one of the earliest marine corps (founded in 1627), France did not maintain a steady corps for much of its history, including during what is arguably its military peak, the reign of Napoleon Bonaparte. The Fusiliers Marins ("Brigade of Marines") was reestablished in 1856 initially to serve aboard naval ships and take part in small-scale landings.

The Fusiliers Marins made their most notable contribution to France's military history during World War I. Among the many battles the Fusiliers took part in were the three Battles of Ypres in western Flanders. The first battle saw some 6,000 Fusiliers defend the city of Diksmuide along the Western Front, where the French soldiers withstood a barrage of German attacks, up to 15 in a single night. While the

Fusiliers were eventually overwhelmed and lost Diksmuide, their valiant fighting helped exhaust the German military en route to the Central Powers' ultimate defeat.

Today, the Fusiliers Marins is composed of around 2,000 troops who serve a variety of roles for the French military and in UN-directed military actions.

The Netherlands

As mentioned earlier, the Koninklijke Nederlandse Corps Mariniers were one of the two first modern marine units and the foremost seafaring troops of the late 17th century. Today, the Corps maintains a force of approximately 2,800 troops that serve under the ultimate authority of the Royal Netherlands Navy. The Corps contains a number of special combat battalions, including two main Marine battalions; infantry companies based in the Netherlands Antilles; and the anti-terrorist Marines Intervention Unit, which was formed in the wake of the hostage crisis of the 1972 Munich Olympic Games. The Corps' domestic operational units are based on Texel Island, in Doorn, and in Den Helder.

Dutch Marines carrying a Norwegian soldier pretending to be injured during joint training exercises. © AP Images

The Corps Mariniers is organized for rapid deployment, particularly on missions run under the auspices of the North Atlantic Treaty Organization (NATO). Despite the fact that the Corps was formed in response to the Dutch-English wars of the 17th century, the two countries now work together closely, with operational units of the Corps Mariniers fully integrated into three Royal Marines commando brigades to form the joint United Kingdom-Netherlands Landing Force.

Russia

As one of the biggest countries in the world—by both size and population—Russia would seem to be an ideal candidate for a large and thriving branch of Marines. However, the Russian Navy has historically emphasized submarine warfare, which naturally placed less importance on ship-based infantry. The Russian version of a marine corps is the Naval Infantry, which is fully integrated into the Russian Navy. Also known as the "Black Berets" for their signature headgear, the Naval Infantry is, though small (approximately 12,000 active soldiers), an elite fighting force.

THE HISTORY OF MARINES AROUND THE WORLD

Members of the Russian Naval Infantry, in their signature black berets, marching through Red Square in Moscow, Russia. © AP Images

The Naval Infantry was founded by Tsar Peter I on Nov. 16, 1705, to serve on his newly created Baltic fleet. The Infantry served ashore and at sea, with a large proportion serving in the Russian fleet that operated within the Mediterranean Sea during the 18th century. During the country's major conflicts of the late 19th and early 20th centuries (namely the Crimean War, the Russo-Japanese War, and World War I), the relatively small Naval Infantry was reinforced by naval troops.

The Naval Infantry was dissolved after the Russian Revolution of 1917 and was only re-formed in 1939 when the 1st Separate Naval Infantry Brigade was created to aid the Soviet Union's war with Finland. The rampant conscription that came with World War II left the Naval Infantry with over 100,000 soldiers by war's end in 1945. Those numbers dwindled as the Soviet Union crumbled and today the smaller Naval Infantry primarily conducts high-risk quick-strike attacks and commando raids.

South Korea

Soon after the division between North and South Korea, the latter (officially known as the Republic of Korea) established the Republic of Korea Marine Corps (ROKMC) on April 15, 1949. Unlike most other Marine Corps, the ROKMC is a standalone branch of the Korean military and is only loosely affiliated with the country's Navy. Although only initially consisting of 380 troops, the ROKMC participated in a number of key reconnaissance and suppression actions during the Korean War (1950–53). ROKMC troops also went into Vietnam to fight alongside U.S. soldiers during the Vietnam War (1954–75). Through most of its history, the ROKMC has been involved in border skirmishes with and, defense against, the North Korean military.

The modern ROKMC has been built up to a force of some 25,000 soldiers (which makes it the second-largest Marine force in the world), who are divided into two divisions and one brigade. The ROKMC works closely with the United States Marine Corps, and the two countries routinely conduct joint training exercises.

United Kingdom

The Royal Marines have five primary functions. They supply fighting units for ships of the Royal Navy; provide bands for the navy, both at sea and on shore; man minor landing craft; provide commando, or amphibious, raiding units; and serve as a link between the army and navy during landing operations. The strength of the Royal Marines in the early 2010s was approximately 7,000, just under 25 percent of the Royal Navy's personnel.

NOTABLE MARINE CORPS AROUND THE WORLD

COMMANDO TRAINING CENTRE ROYAL MARINES

The Commando Training Centre Royal Marines (CTCRM) is the main training center for Royal Marine officers, recruits, and reserves. The Centre is located in Lympstone in the county of Devon in southwest England on a 77-acre campus. CTCRM, then known as the Royal Marines Reserve Depot, was founded in 1939 in the British military build-up before World War II and was originally intended for the training of reservists. In 1941 the camp became known as Depot Royal Marines Lympstone and, at the peak of wartime activity, was training 800 marines per month for service. The camp was given its current name in 1970.

Royal Marine recruits of the CTCRM at the River Exe Estuary in England, participating in the Mud Run, the most grueling portion of the centre's 32-week course. Rex Featuures via AP Images

67

COMMANDO TRAINING CENTRE ROYAL MARINES
(CONTINUED)

The commando training program takes place over 32 weeks, while the officer training takes 64 weeks, and approximately 1,200 recruits enter CTCRM each year. CTCRM consists of three training wings: Command Wing (where all officers and NCOs are trained), Commando Training Wing (which trains all recruits and reservists), and Specialist Wing (where around 70 percent of all Royal Marines specialists are trained). Upon completion of the CTCRM program, Royal Marines are given a much-coveted green beret to signify their accomplishment.

The marine establishment is divided into two groups, one based at Portsmouth and the other at Plymouth. The Portsmouth Group directs the sea training of the troops, while the Plymouth Group is in charge of coordinating land combat training. The Plymouth Group operates the Commando School at Bickleigh and the Infantry Training Centre at Lympstone. Recruits are trained at Deal in Kent, and officers attend the Commando Training Centre Royal Marines at Lympstone. Women serving in the Corps are assigned from the Women's Royal Naval Service (WRENS).

A member of the royal family serves as captain general of the marines. The position has been held by Prince Philip, duke of Edinburgh, since the coronation of Elizabeth II. The highest officer on active duty is the commandant general, who has his headquarters in London at the Royal Marine Office.

Since World War II the principal operating unit of the Royal Marines has been the Commando Brigade. Commandos are trained as shock troops for hit-and-run raids on enemy territory. The Brigade has served in Hong Kong, Palestine, Malaya, and Cyprus. They formed the amphibious assault spearhead in the Suez Crisis of 1956. The Brigade often operates from commando carriers, a British version of the United States Navy's helicopter assault ships.

CHAPTER 6

THE UNITED STATES MARINE CORPS

Their hymn declares that they have fought "from the halls of Montezuma to the shores of Tripoli," referring to exploits by the United States Marine Corps in the Mexican War and in campaigns against the Barbary pirates of North Africa. During the more than 200 years of their history, United States Marines have seen combat in all parts of the world and have been at the forefront of danger in every war the United States has fought with other nations.

ORGANIZATION

The Marine Corps is a self-contained combat force within the Department of the Navy. The authorized strength of the Corps in the late 20th century was 20 percent of that allowed the Navy. (It was about 200,000 in the early 2010s.) The Corps is composed of two Fleet Marine Forces, one posted in the Atlantic and the other in the Pacific. The Atlantic force is based at Norfolk, Va., and

Rendering of the flag of the United States Marine Corps. Atlaspix/Shutterstock.com

the Pacific force has its headquarters at Pearl Harbor, Hawaii.

In addition to supporting the fleet, Marine detachments serve on large warships. In peacetime they provide garrisons to protect Navy yards and other shore facilities. There is also a United States Marine Band that plays for many presidential events and gives public concerts. Overseas, Marines are stationed at embassies and legations to

THE HISTORY OF MARINES AROUND THE WORLD

RECRUIT TRAINING

Prospective enlisted United States Marines undergo 12 weeks of intense preparation known simply as Recruit Training. At Marine bases in either Parris Island or San Diego, recruits are first issued gear, given medical examinations, take a basic strength test (consisting of pull-ups/arm-hangs, crunches, and a timed run), and are assigned to a drill instructor. Over the remainder of the training, the recruits are taught a number of skills, including hand-to-hand combat, shooting, and rappelling in a strictly regimented schedule.

A Marine Corps recruit crawling on her back under barbed wire during the Crucible, the arduous test recruits take towards the end of their training. Stephen Morton/Getty Images

> The key moment of training comes in the final phase, known as the Crucible, which is an incredibly rigorous exercise that tests a recruit's skills, conditioning, and willpower that takes place over 54 continuous hours. Once a recruit finishes the Crucible, he or she receives the Marine Corps Emblem (an eagle standing atop a globe that is intersected by an anchor) and is addressed as a "Marine" for the first time. After recruit training, infantry marines enter a 59-day course known as Infantry Training Battalion while non-infantry marines are enrolled in the 29-day Marine Combat training Battalion before moving on to their respective school of the Military Occupational Specialty.

protect American interests and lives in times of danger. (Several marines were among the hostages held in Iran after the takeover of the United States Embassy at Tehran, Iran, in 1979.)

The Marine Corps is directed by a commandant, a four-star general who reports to the secretary of the Navy. The commandant sits as a member of the Joint Chiefs of Staff. The commandant is not part of the command structure of the chief of naval operations, but there is always close cooperation between the two.

Applicants for the Marine Corps must be from 17 to 28 years old. The usual period of enlistment is from three to five years. Male recruits living east of the Mississippi River are sent to Parris Island, S.C., for training and those who live west of the river go to San Diego, Calif. (All female recruits train at Parris Island regardless of where they live.) This basic training is followed by a shorter period of advanced schooling in small-unit tactics and weaponry at Camp Lejeune, N.C., or Camp Pendleton, Calif.

An integral part of the Corps is the Marine Corps Reserve, established during World War I. Today's Organized Marine Corps Reserve numbers about 40,000. It includes the 4th Marine Division/4th Marine Aircraft Wing. Reservists train two days per month and for two weeks each summer. By mobilizing the reserve, the Corps can increase its strength by about one-fifth within weeks.

The United States Marine Corps Women's Reserve was established in 1943. Its members perform many duties in the mainland United States and Hawaii to release men for combat service. Women have been part of the regular Marine Corps since 1948, when Congress passed the Women's Armed Services Integration Act. Woman recruits train at Parris Island, and those seeking to

WOMEN IN THE UNITED STATES MARINE CORPS

Although the United States Marine Corps Women's Reserve was founded during World War II, women began serving in the Marines during the previous World War. The first female Marine was Opha Mae Johnson, who enlisted in the Marine Corps Reserve on Aug. 13, 1918. She was joined by over 300 other women who served domestically during the war. While the women were not sent overseas to fight, they did clerical work that freed up men to go serve in Europe.

Today, there are nearly 14,000 women in the United States Marine Corps. They make up a much smaller percentage of that branch than women do in other branches of the American armed forces: only about 7 percent of Marines are women, compared to between 13 percent and 19 percent of the other branches. Women in all branches of the military were restricted from combat roles until January 2013, when Secretary of Defense Leon Panetta

Opha Mae Johnson, the first female United States Marine. The United States Marine Corps

WOMEN IN THE UNITED STATES MARINE CORPS (CONTINUED)

ended the official ban on female Marines taking part in artillery and infantry roles. Though controversial to some, the lifting of the ban was also hailed by other factions as a long-overdue step in creating equal opportunities for both sexes, as well as an acknowledgment of the realities of the battlefield, where women have been pressed into active service for decades.

become commissioned officers go to school at Quantico, Va.

The United States Marine Corps Forces Special Operations Command (MARSOC) began operations in 2006 and comprises the Marines' special-operations expeditionary forces who take part in unconventional warfare across the globe, with a focus on counterterrorism. MARSOC is based in Camp LeJeune, N.C., and consists of approximately 2,600 troops and commanders. The Command was formed in order to give the Marines a more fluid fighting unit to engage in the nontraditional combat that became increasingly prevalent in the 21st century, particularly after the terrorist attacks of Sept. 11, 2001.

SEMPER FIDELIS

Semper fidelis (frequently shortened to "*Semper fi*") was adopted as the United States Marine Corps motto in 1883. The phrase is used as a reminder to stay ever-faithful to one's mission and is also meant to evoke a life-long bond that a marine is meant to have with his or her unit, the Corps, and the country. There is also an additional slogan for Marine officers: *Ductus exemplo*, which means "to lead by example" and is the official motto of the Officer Candidates School.

The United States Marine Corps is not the first or only group to use the motto *Semper fidelis*. It has been a popular phrase on families' coats of arms for centuries and has been adopted by numerous schools and military units in the United States and abroad. The first documented use of *Semper fidelis* as a motto for a city comes from 1588, when Queen Elizabeth I suggested its use for Exeter as recognition for that city's contribution to the English fleet that repelled the Spanish Armada.

There is no separate military academy for Marines as there is for the other service branches. Most individuals who wish to make a career in the Marine Corps attend the Naval Academy at Annapolis, Md., though it is also possible to attend the Military Academy at West Point, N.Y., or the Air Force Academy at Colorado

Springs, Colo. Officers go for further training to the school at Quantico.

The Marine motto is *Semper fidelis*, meaning "always faithful." The term "leathernecks" comes from the black leather collars the Marines used to wear, probably to protect their necks from swords and cutlasses. A combined globe, eagle, and anchor forms the Corps emblem.

Many historic relics and souvenirs of the Corps are housed in the Marine Corps Museum at Quantico. One of its proudest possessions is the United States flag that Marines raised atop Mount Suribachi on the island of Iwo Jima during World War II. A bronze sculpture commemorating the event stands in Arlington National Cemetery.

Technology

Like the other branches of the modern American military, the Marine Corps is flush with government funding, which produces the latest in technological innovation. From sailing ships with wooden hulls to radar-evading nuclear-powered submarines, the Marine Corps has been on the front line of advancing military technology.

Vehicles

While ostensibly a maritime fighting force, the United States Marine Corps of course participates in actions on land as well. The most common vehicle used in ground campaigns is the High Mobility Multipurpose Wheeled Vehicle (HMMWV; more commonly known as a Humvee). The HMMWV has been in use since the 1980s but rose to prominence for its role in the Persian Gulf War, which led to the production of a civilian version of the Humvee under the brand name Hummer. The versatile vehicle has been used for troop transport, for carrying armaments, as a mobile command center, and as an ambulance, among many other functions.

In addition to the Humvee, Marine Corps troops on the ground also use Mine Resistant Ambush Protected Vehicles (MRAPs), which are becoming more popular in the 21st century for their resistance to the Improvised Explosive Devices (IEDs) that are increasingly common in modern war zones. Marine Corps soldiers utilize a number of heavier ground vehicles, including tanks, armored troop transports, and path-clearing Assault Breacher Vehicles.

An M1A1 Abrams tank, one of the ground vehicles used by the United States Marine Corps. Marines work on the tank during an exercise in South Korea. Jung Yeon-Je/AFP/Getty Images

One of the signature vehicles of the Marine Corps is the amphibious assault vehicle (AAV). The AAV is an armed and armored military vehicle designed to deliver assault troops and their equipment from ship to shore under combat conditions. Marines frequently used AAVs in battles during the Iraq War.

U.S. Marines lying in front of an amphibious assault vehicle (AAV) during a joint landing operation with the South Korean Marines. Chung Sung-Jun/Getty Images

Aircraft

The United States Air Force is, naturally, the predominant military force associated with aircraft, but the Marine Corps also uses a great number of jets, propeller-driven planes, and helicopters. The primary purpose of aircraft in Marine engagements is to provide close air support to ground troops. Two aircraft are particularly useful in this respect: the AH-1 Super Cobra/Viper helicopter and F/A-18 Hornet fighter jet. The latter is also noted for its versatility, as it can be quickly modified for use in either fighter or attack missions, including enemy air defense suppression, reconnaissance, and fighter escort.

Other notable aircraft in the current Marine arsenal are the AV-8B Harrier II jet, which was the first VSTOL (vertical/short takeoff and landing) jet in Corps history; the C-130J Super Hercules, a massive (90 feet [27 meters] long), propeller-powered airplane that is used for transporting Marines and cargo over long distances; and the MV-22 Osprey, a hybridized helicopter with propellers mounted on wings so that it has the speed and distance-coverage of an airplane and the maneuverability of a helicopter. Recent additions to the aerial arsenal of the Corps are the various Unmanned Aircraft Systems (UAS; often referred to as "drones") that can be piloted remotely and which rose to prominence during the 2010s as a means of retaliating against—and preventatively attacking—terrorists hiding in remote or inaccessible locations.

HISTORY OF THE UNITED STATES MARINE CORPS

CHAPTER 7

The present Marine Corps was established by an act of Congress on July 11, 1798. The Corps, however, celebrates Nov. 10, 1775, as its founding date. It was on that day that the Continental Congress authorized the formation of two battalions of Marines. The first commissioned officer, Capt. Samuel Nicholas, recruited many of this first group in the historic Tun Tavern near Philadelphia. The first Marines sailed with the new American fleet under Esek Hopkins in 1776 and stormed British forts on New Providence Island in the Bahamas. They captured 600 barrels of gunpowder needed by the colonial army.

On Christmas night in 1776 Marines supported George Washington when he crossed the Delaware River to surprise the Hessians in New Jersey. In the naval battles of the American Revolution they fought on the decks of John Paul Jones's *Ranger* and other vessels. Since then, Marines have served in all the wars of the United States, and they

Esek Hopkins, Commander in Chief of the Continental Navy in 1776, on board his ship with his crew. Some of the earliest American Marines sailed with Hopkins and served in other capacities during the American Revolution. Stock Montage/Archive Photos/Getty Images

have executed more than 300 landings on foreign shores.

United States Marine Corps in the 19th Century

After the war the Continental Marines and the Navy were both deactivated. The peril of international events, especially the wars between France and Britain, soon called for reactivation. The Marines and Navy were sent into action immediately during the undeclared naval war with France (1798–1801). During the next century they fought in the Tripolitan War (1801–05), the War of 1812, the Creek and Seminole wars (1836–42), the Mexican War (1846–48), and the American Civil War. During the Civil War the Confederacy established its own Marine units on March 16, 1861. Union Marines fought at Bull Run, on the Mississippi River, and in all the amphibious landings of the Navy along the Confederate coast.

In the Tripolitan War the Marines crossed the northeastern Sahara in Africa afoot and on camel to attack and defeat the Barbary pirates at Tripoli. Over Derna they hoisted

THE HISTORY OF MARINES AROUND THE WORLD

Ships commanded by Matthew C. Perry on his expedition to Japan. Marines accompanied Commodore Perry on his journey. Photos.com/Thinkstock

the Stars and Stripes, and for the first time the United States flag flew above a fortress in the Old World. In 1821 they cleared the Caribbean Sea of pirates as well.

Between wars in the 19th century the Marines landed in the South Seas, China, Japan, Korea, Panama, Uruguay, Paraguay, Egypt, Mexico, Cuba, the Arctic, Formosa (Taiwan), Argentina, Chile, Greenland, Haiti, Nicaragua, and the Samoan Islands. These were not all combat missions. They were with Commodore Matthew Perry when he opened Japan to United States trade in 1854.

OCCUPATION OF HAITI

From 1915 to 1934 Haiti was occupied by United States Marines. The United States claimed that its action was justified under the Monroe Doctrine (the right of the United States to prevent European intervention in the Western Hemisphere) as well as on humanitarian grounds. However, many Haitians believed that the Marines had really been sent to protect U.S. investments and to establish a base to protect the approaches to the Panama Canal. Haiti signed a treaty with the United States—originally for 10 years but later extended—establishing U.S. financial and political domination. In 1918, in an election supervised by the Marines, a new constitution was introduced that permitted foreigners to own land in Haiti.

One effect of the Marine occupation was the nominal reestablishment of the mulatto elite's control of the government. Black Haitians, in contrast, felt that they were excluded from public office and subjected to racist indignities at the hands of the Marines, including the corvée (statute labor, or forced labor for public works); in response, peasant *cacos* (guerrillas) carried out a series of attacks. The Marines' public works program included building new health clinics and sewerage systems, but most Haitians felt that the Marines' efforts were inadequate.

In October 1930 Haitians chose a national assembly for the first time since 1918. It elected as president Sténio Joseph Vincent. In August 1934 U.S. Pres. Franklin D. Roosevelt withdrew the Marines; however, the United States maintained direct fiscal control until 1941 and indirect control over Haiti until 1947.

United States Marine Corps in the Early 20th Century

Following the Spanish-American War of 1898, the Marines saw active duty in the Philippine Insurrection (1899–1902), in the Boxer Rebellion in China (1900), in Cuba (1906–09), in Nicaragua (1912), in Veracruz, Mexico, (1914), in Haiti (1915–34), and in the Dominican Republic (1916–24).

During World War I the 4th Marine Brigade fought in France at Belleau Wood, Soissons, St. Mihiel, Blanc Mont, and the Meuse-Argonne. The 1st Marine Aviation Force flew bombing, fighter, and tactical air-support missions.

As early as 1921 the United States was concerned about a war with Japan in the Pacific. The Marine Corps began its development of modern amphibious warfare. The Corps worked closely with the Navy to evolve the amphibious assault procedures ultimately put to use in World War II. The new tactics were given ample chance to prove themselves during assaults on Guadalcanal (the first United States

BATTLE OF BELLEAU WOOD

From June 1 to June 26, 1918, the forest known as Belleau Wood near the Marne River (about 55 miles [90 km] northeast of Paris) became the site of one of the most important battles of World War I and the first major test of the United States Marine Corps. The United States sent 8,000 Marines along with hundreds of Army soldiers and supporting Navy medical corpsmen to fortify the French resistance to the encroaching German Army. The opposing sides fought in claustrophobic woods and in nearby villages, which led to confusion and poor communication for both the Allies and the Central Powers.

A surge of Marines into volleys of machine-gun fire on June 6 led to the Allies capturing the key Hill 142, but also resulted in

U.S. Marines at the Battle of Belleau Wood, a World War I battle that took place in France in 1918. Everett Collection/SuperStock

THE HISTORY OF MARINES AROUND THE WORLD

BATTLE OF BELLEAU WOOD (CONTINUED)

the largest single-day casualty count in Corps history up to that point: over 1,000 Marines were lost that day. The American forces finally defeated the Germans on June 26—a victory that helped turn the tide of the war by both its strategic importance and by the differing effects on morale the hard-fought battle had on the opposing sides. The Marines' fierce fighting at Belleau Wood gave rise to the reputation for the toughness and dedication of American Marines that in large part exists to this day.

offensive in World War II), Bougainville, Tarawa, Roi-Namur, Eniwetok, New Britain, Tinian, Guam, Peleliu, Iwo Jima, and Okinawa. The Iwo Jima assault cost the Marines about 20,000 casualties, the highest toll of any engagement in their history. By war's end in 1945 the Corps included six divisions, four air wings, and supporting troops. Its top strength during the war reached 485,113, of whom more than 90 percent served in combat.

In the years immediately after the war, the Marines developed an amphibious "vertical envelopment" concept, using assault

BATTLE OF IWO JIMA

The Battle of Iwo Jima was the site of one of the most iconic moments in U.S. Marine history: the raising of the American flag over Mount Suribachi by Marine troops after the Allied victory, which was captured in a famous photograph. The battle for possession of the strategically important Pacific islands took place between February 19 and March 26, 1945. Three United States Marine divisions landed on the Japanese-controlled island in February following

Five U.S. Marines and a Navy corpsman planting the American flag on Mount Suribachi on the island of Iwo Jima after their success in a battle against Japan. The image is one of the most iconic in American history and the inspiration for the U.S. Marine Corps War Memorial.
© AP Images

THE HISTORY OF MARINES AROUND THE WORLD

BATTLE OF IWO JIMA (CONTINUED)

weeks of preliminary bombing. However, the bombing had little impact on the Japanese defenders, who had entrenched themselves within Iwo Jima's intricate cave system.

A month of intense fighting finally ended after American Marines captured the two highest spots on the island: Mount Suribachi in the south and what the U.S. soldiers named "Meatgrinder Hill" in the north. The 36-day campaign resulted in 26,000 American casualties (6,800 dead)—the greatest single-action loss in Corps history—and almost 19,000 Japanese casualties, nearly all of which were deaths from either enemy fire or ritual suicide. Some Japanese soldiers hid out in the island's caves rather than surrender, with the last holdouts ultimately surrendering in 1949. The capture of the island gave the Allies a key base for aircraft en route to bombing raids on the Japanese mainland.

helicopters as landing craft and aircraft carriers as transport. The purpose was to achieve a more flexible, widely dispersed, and rapid landing attack than had been previously possible. These tactics were put to use during the Korean and Vietnam wars and were adopted by the Army as well.

United States Marine Corps From c. 1950 to c. 2000

After World War II Marine strength dropped below 100,000. When the Korean War broke out in 1950, the corps was enlarged to about 250,000. The Marines were the first reinforcements dispatched from the United States to aid Army troops already in place. From 1951 to 1953 ground and aviation units played a major part in the hard-fought but indecisive battles along the 38th parallel dividing North from South Korea.

The Chosin Reservoir campaign early in the Korean War, was part of the Chinese Second Offensive (November–December 1950) to drive the United Nations out of North Korea. The Chosin Reservoir campaign was directed mainly against the 1st Marine Division of the U.S. X Corps, which had disembarked in eastern North Korea and moved inland in severe winter weather to a mountainous area near the reservoir. The campaign succeeded in forcing the entire X Corps to evacuate to South Korea, but the Chinese did not achieve their particular objective of isolating and

U.S. Marines lying in snow with rifles near the Chosin Reservoir in South Korea, during the Chosin Reservoir campaign in 1950. © AP Images

destroying the 1st Marine Division. Instead, in a deliberate retrograde movement that has become one of the most-storied exploits in Marine Corps lore, the Marines turned and fought their way down a narrow vulnerable road through several mountain passes and a bridged chasm until they reached transport ships waiting at the coast.

In March 1965 the 3rd Marine Division became the first United States ground unit

LEWIS PULLER

Lewis "Chesty" Puller (1898–1971) was arguably the most-lauded American Marine of all time. He attended the Virginia Military Institute but left the school to join the Marines in an attempt to join the fighting in World War I. While he never served in that war, he did see action in both World War II and the Korean War. Puller was known for his tendency to expose himself to enemy fire in order to walk along the lines of his troops to shout encouragement and instructions to them. He was promoted to general after just 33 years in the Corps, an incredibly short period for an enlisted man to rise so far. He served in the Corps for 37 years and is the only marine to ever receive the Navy Cross—the second-highest military award for both the Navy and the Marines—five times.

to be deployed in Vietnam when they landed at Da Nang. Within two years three Marine divisions and supporting aviation had been committed to major combat and pacification operations. To support these units the strength of the Corps was raised to 275,000.

Between wartime activities in Korea and Vietnam the Marines landed in the Tachen Islands, Taiwan, Thailand, and Lebanon in countermeasures to communist pressures in the Cold War. During the 1962 Cuban missile crisis, Marines reinforced the naval base at Guantánamo Bay and surrounded Cuba with floating expeditionary forces. Because the Soviet Union agreed to withdraw its missiles, these forces did not engage in combat. In 1965 Marines landed at Santo Domingo to prevent a rebel takeover of the Dominican Republic.

It was in Lebanon that the Marine Corps experienced its greatest losses after Vietnam. In September 1982 Pres. Ronald Reagan agreed to send Marines to Beirut as part of a peacekeeping force, along with French and Italian servicemen. There were at the time many mutually hostile Arab factions fighting each other. Some were supported by Syria, others by Iran. Remnants of a divided Palestine Liberation Organization were also involved in the fighting. The Marines, unfortunately, were perceived to be partial to Arab Christian militiamen and hostile to Muslim factions.

In March 1983 a Marine patrol was attacked by grenade throwers. On Sunday, October 23, a truck loaded with explosives careened into the Marine compound at the Beirut airport. The explosion killed 239 marines and 58 French servicemen instantly. Not long afterward the peacekeeping force

Two U.S. Marines standing in the rubble of the Marine compound in Beirut after a terrorist bombing attack destroyed it and killed nearly 300 individuals in 1983. Peter Jordan/Time & Life Pictures/Getty Images

was withdrawn, leaving Lebanon to its seemingly interminable civil war.

The Marine Corps' participation in the Persian Gulf War has already been noted in this book, but that was not the only action Marines saw during the 1990s. Marines played a key role in the U.S.-led intervention into war-torn Somalia in 1992. On December 9 of that year, the 15th Marine Expeditionary Unit took part in an unopposed amphibious landing at the Somali capital of Mogadishu, becoming the first of over 35,000 international troops to enter Somalia during the Somali Civil War. The Marines' stay in Somalia was not as benign as its entrance, as soldiers from the Corps took part in many bloody battles during the fourteen months that U.S. forces occupied Somalia.

The United States Marine Corps in the Present

Since the dawn of the new millennium, the United States Marine Corps has undergone tremendous change, despite the comparatively short timeframe. Of course, a signal event in American history took place soon

A U.S. Marine on patrol in Iraq stops to examine a suspicious box in the road. John Moore/Getty Images

after the turn of the century when terrorists crashed airliners into the World Trade Center towers in New York City and the Pentagon in Washington, D.C., on Sept. 11, 2001. The attacks precipitated massive changes to much of American society, including the Marine Corps, as 9/11 instituted the so-called "Global War on Terror" and kicked off a worldwide campaign by the U.S. military to combat terrorism.

As a result, Marines were deployed to the wars in Afghanistan and Iraq as well as to areas that fomented terrorists (or had the potential to) the world over. The secrecy and fast action necessitated by the covert operations needed to root out terrorists on foreign soil were tailor-made for the Marine Corps. Consequently, the Corps created an infantry unit called the Anti-Terrorism Battalion that existed from 2001 to 2007 with troops specially trained for crisis response, intelligence and counterintelligence operations, and urban warfare.

Another massive change to the Corps came when the "Don't Ask, Don't Tell" (DADT) policy was ended throughout the American armed forces. DADT was instituted in 1993 to make official a longstanding informal ban on openly homosexual troops serving in the U.S. military. The repeal was passed by the U.S. Congress in mid-December 2010, signed into law by Pres. Barack Obama on the 22nd, and officially implemented on Sept. 21, 2011. The abolition of DADT was controversial, but surveys done one year after the repeal show that over 75 percent of Marines felt that the removal of DADT had either no impact or a positive impact on the Corps.

CONCLUSION

While marines play different roles (and even take on different names) from country to country, they are unified by a fundamental tie to the sea. But the marines of today have transcended that connection and can be called on to do battle anywhere; it is this versatility that truly sets the marines apart. Some marine corps are part of a navy, some are part of the army, and some are independent, but they each consist of all-purpose troops who can fight in any of the other military branches' nominal areas of specialization at a moment's notice. As the United States Marine Corps' famous hymn puts it, marines are the soldiers who can be found fighting "from the Halls of Montezuma to the shores of Tripoli."

GLOSSARY

amphibious Relating to or adapted for both land and water; also, executed by coordinated action of land, sea, and air forces organized for invasion.

artillery The part of a military force that uses large guns to shoot over a great distance.

berm A mound or wall of earth or sand.

cease-fire An agreement to stop fighting a war for a period of time so that a permanent agreement can be made to end the war.

commando A military unit trained and organized as shock troops especially for hit-and-run raids into enemy territory; also, the member of such a unit.

corvée Labor exacted in lieu of taxes by public authorities especially for highway construction or repair.

drone A military aircraft that is guided autonomously, by remote control, or both and that carries sensors, target designators, offensive ordnance, or electronic transmitters designed to interfere with or destroy enemy targets.

galley A short crescent-shaped seagoing ship of classical antiquity propelled chiefly by oars though generally having a mast carrying an oblong sail.

garrison A military post; also, the troops stationed at a garrison.

Greek fire An incendiary composition used in warfare by the Byzantine Greeks that is said to have burst into flames on wetting.

guerrilla Of or relating to an irregular military force fighting small-scale, limited actions, in concert with an overall political-military strategy, against conventional military forces; also, a member of such a force.

infantry Troops trained, armed, and equipped to fight on foot.

reconnaissance Of or relating to an exploratory military survey of enemy territory.

retrograde Moving, occurring, or performed in a backward direction.

sharpshooter A proficient marksman.
vertical envelopment Envelopment of a military enemy from the air (as with troops dropped by parachute or landed by gliders, helicopters, or airplanes) usually to seize key objectives in the enemy's rear.
war of attrition Warfare characterized by one side weakening and gradually defeating an enemy through constant attacks and continued pressure over a long period of time.

FOR MORE INFORMATION

Marines Corps Heritage Foundation (MCHF)
3800 Fettler Park Drive, Suite 104
Dumfries, VA 22025
(888) 315-1775
Web site: http://www.marineheritage.org
The MCHF is an organization tasked with completion of the Marine Corps Heritage Center, a project closely associated with the National Museum of the Marine Corps dedicated to raising funding and awareness of United States Marine Corps history. The MCHF offers several prestigious awards for historical research on the Marines or accurate representations of their lives in the arts, as well as fellowships for post-graduate level work in Marine Corps history.

National Museum of the Marine Corps
18900 Jefferson Davis Highway

FOR MORE INFORMATION

Triangle, VA 22172
(877) 635-1775
Web site: http://www.usmcmuseum.com
The National Museum of the Marine Corps collects and preserves the material history of the United States Marine Corps, combining permanent exhibits on major conflicts involving the Marines with collections-based research and publications to advance knowledge, training, and awareness of Marine history and accomplishments.

Navy League of the United States (NLUS)
2300 Wilson Boulevard, Suite 200
Arlington, VA 22201
(800) 356-5760
Web site: http://www.navyleague.org
The NLUS was founded in 1902 to provide a voice to civilians supporting the United States Navy, Marine Corps, and Coast Guard. It seeks to develop the morale of armed forces personnel and the public, promote education and awareness of the Sea Services of the U.S. Armed Forces, and encourage youth involvement through its Naval Sea Cadets Corps, Junior R.O.T.C., and Young Marines programs.

Navy & Marine Living History Association (NMLHA)
41 Kelley Boulevard
North Attleboro, MA 02760
Web site: http://www.navyandmarine.org
The NMLHA is a nonprofit corporation that promotes the study of the United States' nautical history and the ship companies of the United States Navy and Marine Corps. It provides naval historical references, bibliographic references on ships, and access to newsletters and museums from associated organizations.

Parris Island Museum
Building #111
Marine Corps Recruit Depot
Parris Island, SC 29905
(843) 228-2951
Web site: http://parrisislandmuseum.com
Established in 1990 on the Marine Corps Recruit Depot of Parris Island, S.C., the Parris Island Museum details the history of Port Royal as a key military base since the American Revolution. Converted into a Marines Corps base after the Spanish-American War, some of the earliest artifacts from the history of the United

For More Information

States Marine Corps are housed there.
United States Marine Corps History Division
3078 Upshur Avenue
Quantico, VA 22134
(703) 432-4874
Web site: https://www.mcu.usmc.mil
The U.S. Marine Corps History Division is tasked with researching and recording the official written history of the United States Marine Corps. Members of its Field History Branch and its Historical Reference Branch collect relevant maps, artifacts, documents, and plans and transmit them into official publications for public use as reference source material.

Web Sites

Due to the changing nature of Internet links, Rosen Educational Services has developed an online list of Web sites related to the subject of this book. This site is updated regularly. Please use this link to access the list:

http://www.rosenlinks.com/armed/marine

FOR FURTHER READING

Alberti, Bruno. *USMC Uniforms & Equipment 1941-1945*. Havertown, PA: Histoire and Collections, 2007.

Cook, Colleen Ryckert. *Your Career in the Marines*. New York: Rosen Publishing, 2011.

Dolan, Edward F. *Careers in the U.S. Marine Corps*. New York: Benchmark Books, 2009.

Gitlin, Martin. *Operation Desert Storm*. Edina, MN: ABDO, 2009.

Horner, David & Robert John O'Neill. *World War II: The Pacific*. New York: Rosen, 2010.

Montana, Jack. *Marines*. Broomall, PA: Mason Crest, 2010.

Orr, Tamra B. *USMC Special Reaction Teams*. New York: Rosen Central, 2008.

Poolos, Jamie. *Black Ops and Other Special Missions of the U.S. Marine Corps Special Operations Command*. New York: Rosen Central, 2012.

FOR FURTHER READING

Sodaro, Craig. *The U.S. Marines Special Operations Regiment: The Missions*. North Mankato, MN: Capstone Press, 2012.

Varble, Derek. *The Suez Crisis*. New York: Rosen Publishing, 2008.

INDEX

A

Afghanistan War, 55, 100
Africa, 28, 29, 70, 85
AH-1 Super Cobra/Viper helicopters, 82
Allied Powers, 41, 42, 43, 46, 89, 91, 92
al-Qaeda, 55
American Civil War, 36–38, 85
American Revolution, 25, 30–31, 83
amphibious assault vehicles (AAVs), 80
Argentina, 52–53, 86
Arlington National Cemetery, 78
Asquith, H.H., 43
Assault Breacher Vehicles, 79
Australia, 43
AV-8B Harrier II jets, 82

B

Bahamas, 83
Banana Wars, 39–40
Belgium, 41
Belleau Wood, Battle of, 88, 89–90
Black Berets, 63
Blanc Mont, Battle of, 43, 88
Bougainville, Battle of, 90
Boxer Rebellion, 88
Brazil, 23
Brown, John, 36
Bull Run, Battle of, 85
Bunker Hill, Battle of, 31
Byzantine Empire, 11, 19, 21

C

Central Powers, 41, 61, 89
Charles V, 21
Chile, 86

INDEX

China, 47, 48, 50, 58–60, 86, 88, 93
Chinese Second Offensive, 93
Chosin Reservoir, Battle of, 48, 93
Churchill, Winston, 43
Cold War, 95
Commando Training Centre Royal Marines (CTCRM), 67–68
communism, 50, 58, 60, 95
C-130J Super Hercules planes, 82
Confederate Army, 36, 38, 85
Continental Congress, 83
Creek War, 85
Crimean War, 25, 64
Crucible, the, 73
Cuba, 40, 86, 88, 95–96
Cuban missile crisis, 95–96
Cyprus, 69

D

Da Nang, 50, 95
D-Day, 46
Denmark, 29
Desert Storm, Operation, 53

Dominican Republic, 88, 96
"Don't Ask, Don't Tell," 100
drone aircraft, 10, 82
Ductus exemplo, 77
Dutch West India Company, 29

E

Egypt, 26, 49, 86
1812, War of, 35, 85
Elizabeth I, 77
Elizabeth II, 69
embassies, 71, 73
Eniwetok, Battle of, 90

F

F/A-18 Hornet fighter jets, 82
Falkland Islands War, 52–53
Fallujah, Battle of, 57
Finland, 65
First Anglo-Dutch War, 28
First Northern War, 29
Formosa, 86
Four Days' Battle, 29
France, 27, 29, 32, 33, 34–35, 43, 44, 46, 49, 50, 60–61, 85, 88, 89, 96
Fusiliers Marins, 60–61

G

galley warfare, 14, 15–16, 21
Gallipoli Campaign, 41, 42–43
Germany, 9, 41, 43, 44, 46, 60, 61, 89, 90
Gibraltar, Great Siege of, 23, 31–33
"Global War on Terror," 100
Greek fire, 21
Greenland, 86
Guadalcanal, Battle of, 44, 47, 88
Guam, Battle of, 90
Guantánamo Bay, 96
guerilla warfare, 40

H

Haiti, 40, 86, 87, 88
Harpers Ferry, 36
Herodotus, 19
Hessians, 83
Honduras, 40
Hong Kong, 69
Hopkins, Esek, 83
Hue, Battle of, 50
Humvees, 79

I

Improvised Explosive Devices (IEDs), 79
India, 22

Infanteria de Marina, 21–22
Iran, 73, 96
Iraq, 53, 55, 56–57, 80, 100
Iraq War, 56–57, 80, 100
Israel, 49
Istanbul, 42
Italy, 46, 96
Iwo Jima, Battle of, 44, 78, 90, 91–92

J

Japan, 13, 26, 46, 47, 64, 86, 88, 91–92
Johnson, Opha Mae, 75
Jones, John Paul, 83
Jutland, Battle of, 25

K

Kandahar International Airport, 55
Khe Sanh, 50
Koninklijke Nederlandse Corps Mariniers, 19, 26–29, 61–63
Korean War, 26, 47–48, 66, 92, 93, 95
Kriegsmarine, 44
Kuwait, 53, 55

L

leathernecks, 78
Lebanon, 95, 96–98
Lejeune, Camp, 74, 76

INDEX

M

Malaya, 69
marines corps
  around the world, 58–69
  command structure, 17–18
  development of, 13–16
  earliest corps, 19–29
  gays in, 11, 100–101
  overview of, 8–11
  reservists, 67, 68, 74, 75, 76
  what they are, 13–18
  women in the, 11, 68–69, 74–76
Marine Corps Museum, 78
Medway, Raid on the, 27, 29
Meuse-Argonne, Battle of, 88
Mexican War, 70, 85
Mexico, 70, 85, 86, 88
Middle East, 49
Midway, Battle of, 47
military engagements, major, 39–57
Mine Resistant Ambush Protected Vehicles (MRAPs), 79
Monroe Doctrine, 87
Munich Olympic Games of 1972, 61
MV-22 Osprey helicopters, 82

N

Napoleon Bonaparte, 34, 60
Napoleonic wars, 23, 25, 34–35
Nasser, Gamal Abdel, 48–49
Navy Cross, 95
Netherlands, the, 16, 19, 26–29, 35, 61–63
New Britain, Battle of, 90
New Zealand, 43
Nicaragua, 40, 86, 88
Nicholas, Samuel, 83
Normandy Invasion, 44, 46
North Atlantic Treaty Organization (NATO), 63
North Korea, 47, 48, 65, 66, 93

O

Obama, Barack, 101
Okinawa, Battle of, 47, 90
Olympic Games, 61
Operation Desert Storm, 53

P

Palestine, 69, 96
Palestine Liberation Organization (PLO), 96

Panama, 40, 86
Panetta, Leon, 75–76
Paraguay, 86
Parris Island, 74
Pearl Harbor, 44, 46, 71
Peleliu, Battle of, 90
Pendleton, Camp, 74
Pentagon, 100
People's Liberation Army (PLA), 58–59, 60
Perry, Matthew, 86
Persian Gulf War, 53–55, 79, 98
Peter I, 64
Philip, Prince, 69
Philippine Insurrection, 88
Philip II, 22
pirates, 22, 28, 70, 85, 86
Pitcairn, John, 31
Polybius, 19
Portugal, 22–23, 28
Protestantism, 22
Puller, Lewis, 95

Q

Quantico (Va.), 76, 78

R

Raid on the Medway, 27, 29
Ranger, 83
Reagan, Ronald, 96
Recon Marines, 51
Republic of Korea Marine Corps (ROKMC), 65–66
Roi-Namur, 90
Roosevelt, Franklin D., 87
Royal Marines, 19, 23–26, 30, 31, 33, 34, 35, 46, 52, 55, 57, 63, 66–69
Russia, 44, 63–65
Russian Revolution of 1917, 65
Russo-Japanese War, 64
Ruyter, Michiel A. de, 26, 28–29

S

Ṣaddām Ḥussein, 56
Saint-Mihiel, Battle of, 88
Samoan Islands, 86
scurvy, 33
Second Anglo-Dutch War, 26, 27, 28, 29
Seebataillon, 41
Seminole Wars, 85
Semper Fidelis, 77, 78
September 11 attacks, 55, 76, 100
Seven Years' War, 25
Sicily, invasion of, 46
Singapore, 26
slavery, 36
Small Wars Operations, 40

INDEX

Soissons, Battle of, 88
Solebay, Battle of, 27, 29
Somalia, 98
South Georgia, 52
South Korea, 65–66, 93
Soviet Union, 39, 47, 50, 65, 96
Spain, 21–22, 23, 28, 32, 33, 40, 77, 88
Spanish-American War, 40, 88
Suez Crisis, 26, 48–49, 69
Sweden, 29
Syria, 96

T

Tachen Islands, 95
Taiwan, 60, 86, 95
Taliban, 55
Tarawa, Battle of, 90
Tet Offensive, 50
Thailand, 95
Third Anglo-Dutch War, 27, 28, 29
38th Parallel, 47, 93
Thucydides, 19
Tinian, Battle of, 90
Trafalgar, Battle of, 35
Tripolitan War, 85–86
Tromp, Maarten, 28
Tun Tavern, 83
Turkey, 42, 43

U

U-boats, 41
Union Army, 36, 38, 85
United Kingdom, 16, 19, 22, 23–26, 27, 29, 30, 31, 32, 33, 34, 35, 41, 43, 46, 49, 52, 56, 57, 63, 66–69, 83, 85
United Kingdom-Netherlands Landing Force, 63
United Nations (UN), 47, 49, 53, 61, 93
Unmanned Aircraft Systems (UAS), 10, 82
Uruguay, 86
U.S. Congress, 74, 83, 101
U.S. Department of the Navy, 70
U.S. Marine Band, 71
U.S. Marine Corps
  emblems, 73, 78
  gays in, 11, 100–101
  history of, 13, 30–31, 46–48, 50–51, 53–55, 83–98
  motto, 77, 78
  organization of, 17–18, 70–78
  recruit training, 72–73
  technology of, 78–82
  today, 98–101
  women in, 11, 74–76

117

U.S. Marine Corps Forces Special Operations Command (MARSOC), 76
U.S. Marine Corps Women's Reserve, 74–76
U.S. Naval Academy, 77

V

vertical envelopment concept, 90, 92
Vietnam War, 50–51, 57, 66, 92, 94–95, 96
Vincent, Sténio Joseph, 87
Virginia Military Institute, 95
VSTOL jets, 82

W

Washington, George, 83
West Indies, 29
West Point, 77
Witt, Johan de, 26
Women's Armed Services Integration Act, 74
Women's Royal Navy Service (WRENS), 69
World Trade Center, 100
World War I, 13, 41–44, 60, 64, 74, 75, 88, 89–90, 95
World War II, 9, 13, 25–26, 44–47, 65, 67, 69, 75, 78, 88, 90, 91–92, 93, 95

X

X Corps, 93

Y

Ypres, Battles of, 60